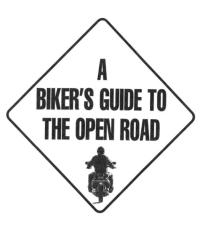

A BIKER'S GUIDE TO THE OPEN ROAD

RIDE IT LIKE YOU STOLE IT

Penny Powers & Chuck Hays

ILLUSTRATED BY ANNE MITCHELL

Gibbs Smith, Publisher
Salt Lake City

First Edition
08 07 06 05 04   10 9 8 7 6 5 4 3 2 1

Published by
Gibbs Smith, Publisher
P.O. Box 667
Layton, UT 84041

Orders: 800.748.5439
www.gibbs-smith.com

Design by Anne Mitchell
Printed and bound in the United States of America

Library of Congress Cataloging-in-Publication Data
Powers, Penny, 1948-
A biker's guide to the open road : ride it like you stole it / by Penny Powers
and Chuck Hays ; illustrated by Anne Mitchell.— 1st ed.
p. cm.
ISBN 1-58685-238-8
1. Motorcycling—Humor. 2 Motorcycles—Humor.
3. Motorcycling—Caricatures and cartoons.
4 Motorcycles—Caricatures and cartoons. I. Hays, Chuck.
II. Title.
PN6231.M744 P68 2004
818'.602—dc22
                        2003023246

To Sylvester H. Roper,
who understood the desire
to be riding free.

One prairie dog
on the road
increases the
pucker factor by two.
As the number of
prairie dogs rises,
the pucker factor
increases
exponentially.

In motorcycling,
the good guys have
names like "Pig,"
"Grizzly," "Horseface,"
and "Slammer."

A biker can tell what part of the country he's in by the taste of the bugs.

Ridin' through
a hailstorm
will make you look
like you've got
chicken pox.

Speed costs money.
How fast is
your wallet?

**Any ride
that did less than
a hundred dollars'
damage to the bike
was a good one.**

Tell a woman she can't do somethin' and she'll kill herself tryin' to prove you wrong.

If you ask someone
whether they want help,
don't get your feelings
hurt if they say
"no."

There are
occassions when
only full-dress leathers
will do.

Never forget
the many bikers
who now ride the
Ultimate Highway
so that you may
ride free today.

**Respect
your elders—
they've seen
a lot more asphalt
than you have.**

The five food groups
of motorcycling:
gas, oil, nicotine,
caffeine, and beer.

**When bikers
throw a party,
they usually invite
300,000 of their
closest friends.**

A biker with a dark-tanned face will have legs as white as winter in North Dakota.

A month on the road—
you're greasy,
sunburned, and tired.

There's also a
negative side.

The thinner your oil,
the easier you'll start
on cold mornings.

There's a
time for ridin'
and a time for
wrenchin'.

Learn to wrench
your own ride.

**The tiniest parts
are always mounted
over the worst place
to drop them.**

Owning three motorcycles won't get you there any faster.

**Never
stop a fistfight
unless they're
getting too close
to the bikes.**

There are eagles
in the mountains and
seagulls by the shore,
and every one of them
has their eye on
your bike.

**Lifestyles
are only romantic
when viewed from
a distance.**

Never tick off
your mechanic.

A
crescent wrench
can double as a
food processor.

There should
always be more
miles on your bike
than your car.

**Mileage is
correctly counted
in number of
engine rebuilds.**

**Before you put on
your chaps,
be sure you have
your pants on.**

**It's not rude to
ask a biker how many
cubic inches
he's got.**

**Good whiskey
is never harmed
by a thousand miles
in a boot flask.**

**Your life
may someday
depend on what
the person in front
of you drank for
breakfast.**

There ain't a more innocent line that'll get you in trouble than "Take me for a ride?"

If you
want to lose
your pretty face,
try sittin' on
someone's bike
without askin'
first.

**The larger the crowd,
the faster you were.**

Don't ride
with any man
who claims to have
survived a tank-slapper
at a hundred miles
an hour.

If you want to be
treated like a badass,
you have to BE a badass . . .

**and if you ARE
a badass,
don't be surprised at
how people treat you.**

A true biker's throttle hand twitches in his sleep.

**Try to make
the campsite
just before the
motorcycle
breaks.**

**Never precede
your motorcycle into
the garage.**

When you find
yourself in a ditch,
the first thing to do
is ease up on the
throttle.

When someone
stops to help you,
pass it on by helping
someone else.

No matter how many tools you carry, you'll need the one you left at home.

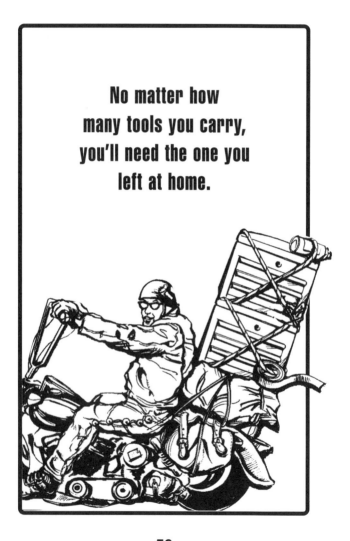

Working in a bike shop
sounds romantic,
until you realize
you'll be workin'
during the riding
season.

A makeshift repair
can sometimes work
better than a
brand new
part.

You wanna be an
old-school rider?
Just wait until the
company quits making
parts for your bike.

When a repair
isn't going well,
be careful of offering
your own opinion.

It takes only
a little dirt to
keep the piston from
going up and down
in the cylinder.

It's not polite
to ask someone
how they got
their nickname.

If she wants some new ink for her birthday, she's a keeper.

**Even a shirt collar
can become a hazard
on the road.**

You know
it's a bad crosswind
when you're scraping
your footpeg on a
straight road.

Backseat riders
should get their
own bikes.

You'll never know
how long you can
ride on reserve
until you run it out
completely.

A biker is an odd
combination of
loner and joiner.

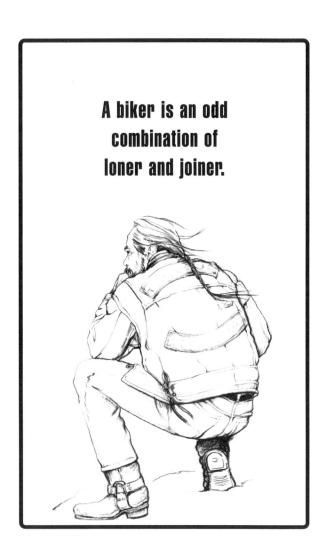

Never ask a biker
why they ride
because you won't
understand the
answer.

Bikers and cowboys are the only people who can feast on beans with impunity.

**Don't
deal a friend false
and then turn
your back.**

Say what you want
about safety—
sometimes you just
want the wind on
your skin and
in your hair.

He may have only
one eye, but he can
snatch a grasshopper
out of the air at 50 mph.

No one
wants to hear
about how to
remove badger guts
from the footpegs
until they need
to do it
themselves.

**The identity of
small rubber parts
becomes apparent only
after the bike
is back together.**

If you put it all back together and it runs beautifully, be afraid— be very afraid.

One person's trash
is another person's
treasure.

A week on
the road together
will tell you more
about his character
than a diamond ring
and a promise.

Some days you'd trade your soul for dry socks.

Nothin'
works better to
keep the rain away
than wearin'
rain gear.

Never ask the pit crew
if they think your
bike should be
faster.

Whatever it is,
go around it.
You can't tell a rock
from cotton candy
at 60 mph.

Before you play poker,
you and everybody else
leave your hardware
with the bartender.

Carry a good knife.
If nothing else,
clean fingernails
might get you into
that motel on a
stormy night.

Never let workin' get in the way of ridin'.

A beautiful custom bike can begin with an idea and a single part.

A diet of
chili and refried
beans can ruin a
motorcycle seat.

There's nothing
like a patch of
wet leaves for leaving
skid marks in your
underwear.

Test a newbie
by askin' about his
muffler bearings.

A construction zone
is no place to test
your throttle.

**Not everything
can be blamed on a
broken speedo cable.
There is always the
ubiquitous damaged
muffler bearing.**

**Milwaukee iron is
one thing that is still
handed down from one
generation to another.**

At least once in your life,
ride to all the towns
that share the name
of the town where
you grew up.

It's all
the same
wind.

If you're lost,
maybe this is where
you should have
been going.

**Don't make
a promise
in the tavern
you can't keep
on the road.**

**Fringe and chrome
reduce your gas
mileage.**

It's easy
to spot an instant
outlaw in the bar or
on the road.

**Carrying spare parts
is a guarantee that
what breaks
will not be one of them.**

**Chrome
don't get you
home.**

Don't use the intercom for telling dirty jokes.

If you're gonna
have a windshield,
cruise control, a stereo,
and a trailer,
you might as well
sell the bike and buy a
Winnebago.

**Always pack
an umbrella—
you never know when
it's gonna rain.**

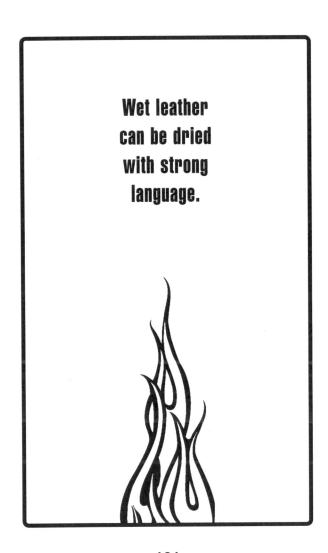

Wet leather
can be dried
with strong
language.

**Remember
your mistakes
as well as your
triumphs.**

**Motorcycle
preachers bless
the bikes *and* the riders.
They know that too many
people forget one or
the other.**

Always take a
bedroll with you
because you never
know where you'll
be tonight.

A big breakfast is fuel for the whole day.

**Happiness is
a gas station with
fresh coffee and
clean bathrooms.**

Remember that some of today's shallow poser-kids may survive to full-fledged geezerhood.

Bikers have so little
respect for authority
that it's almost impossible
to get a given group
to agree on anything.

You can always tell
a biker who lives in the
mountains because
his tires go bald
on the sides.

**Sometimes
the journey ain't
about how fast
you get there.**

Sometimes it is.

**Sometimes needles
actually do fall off the speedometer,
but never when you
want them to.**

You have to be able
to ride fast enough
to keep the raindrops
moving off to the side
edge of your goggles.
Anything less and
you won't be able to
see a thing.

Bikers and tattoos
go together.
Your ink and your ride
should always be clean
when they're new.

Don't take
a fresh rebuild
to the track.

**Celebrate
the happy stuff,
honor the sad stuff.**

He may be fast
in the quarter mile,
but can he go
coast to coast
and still be smilin'
at the end of it?

**Never use
the air cleaner
for putting on your
makeup.**

**Chrome
is my favorite
color.**

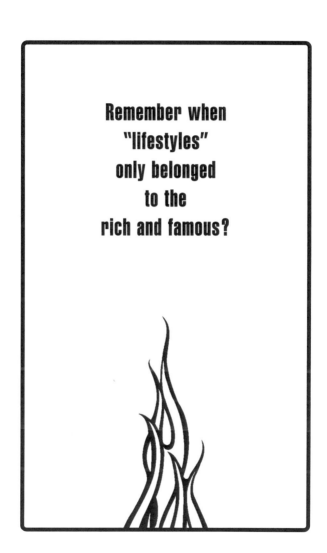

Remember when
"lifestyles"
only belonged
to the
rich and famous?

It's amazing how much good somebody can get out of a simple wave.

It's a sad day
when you have to start
takin' event patches
off your jacket to
make room for another
memory patch.

After a day
alone on the bike,
some people like
to just sit.

Other folks
chatter.

If it's a day-long rain—
ride in it.
If it's a shower—
wait it out.
If you can't tell—
have another tasty
beverage.

**Asphalt
has a personality.
Respect it
and you'll never get to see it
up close.**

**The best
journeys end
with the
thousand-mile
stare.**